The Blessed Path

For information address:

J2B Publishing LLC
4251 Columbia Park Road
Pomfret, MD 20675
www.J2BLLC.com

Printed and bound in the United States of America.

This book is set in Garamond.

ISBN: 978-1-948747-48-6

The Blessed Path

Dorothy A. Simms

J2B PUBLISHING

Reflection

To my husband of fifty-four years and my two children who have been such an inspiration in my life. With love and understanding, they have helped me through the weathering storms of my life. Many of my poems were written as a result of them.

To my family with love and hope, lasting forever.

Table of Contents

Stolen Hearts and Minds

I turned on the news today
So shocking with what
The reporter has to say
Broken hearted mothers
Lost sons and brothers
Pushers dressed in leather
Blood money under cover
Some sat and stewed
Asking what in the hell can we do
It's a shame they say
How people are today
Brothers killing brothers
Men in blue discovers
Scenes at its worst
Young old
such evil they project
don't you understand
There is an ultimate plan
Taking lives away
Two maybe three a day
Open up your heart
Give it all to God
His love is deep inside

Give the straight life a try
It is yours if you try
The word of God will be your guide

Inspirational

If God Wanted Us

If God wanted us
To carry our sins on our shoulder
Jesus would not have carried
The cross on his

God's Way

Goodness - in all that we do
Order - knowing the way
Discipline - being our best regardless of the test

God

God sustained us
He hears our every cry
He is with us through it all
He will never leave our side.

Angels Amongst Us

An old man
With worn out clothes
And a sack on his back
No shoes on his feet
As he lived on the streets
With little or nothing did he eat
As he journeyed for miles
Both day and night
He came to a place
Where the wealthy
Laid stake
To welcome him
No one cared to do
But the smile on his face
Was seen every day
For the holy word of God sustained
Him claimed him
To stand for awhile
O that place of rejection
Remembering all that had been told
Where ever you go my angels
Will show the treasures
Deep in your soul
Though riches you do not possess
My blessings more than gold
My promise everlasting
Just listen and know
My love is everlasting

A Stirring In My Soul

Oh, my Jesus
What a stirring in my soul
I am holding on
To that which you bestowed
Sometimes I sat in wonder
Of olden times past

your blessings everlasting
Hearing my every prayer

O what a stirring
What a stirring in my soul
with hands stretched out
To every weary soul

And each day
With the glory all around
blessings from heaven
where mercy abounds
Oh, I feel a stirring in my soul
One that can't be restrained
to this broken soul
so many have turned away
They go to the darkest place
No rest from day to day
they feel they've failed the test
God hears when we pray
Call his holy name
Be stirred to know his message
God knows all things
Listen
Be stirred to hear his holy voice

Feelings

Loneliness

Where do you go
When loneliness comes your way
While struggling so hard
It just won't go away
When life seems so cold
as lies unfold
And the truth stands still
while a life is ruined
Until it has no will
Loneliness
Where do you go
When it takes your joy
Leaving a sense of fear
O' But for the word of God
His love still abides
No power could ever be

From loneliness
He beckons me
from loneliness because he loves me
and now it has no claim.

Madness

Madness does not care
It leaves its traces everywhere
Behind closed doors it silences joy
It changes lives of little girls and boys
It laughs at intolerance
And scrapes at precious thoughts
Leaving behind its traces
Where sanity vanishes
And happiness lives no more.

The Residue Of Hatred

The residue of hatred
Can be found anywhere
In familiar places
It does not seem to care
It squeezes between two people
At times many more
You will never see its traces
Its truthfulness lives no more
The residue of hatred
Separates
It illuminates darkness
And steals the real love to be
It discriminates
In darkness it feels so very free
Just look around you
And you will see
Such a damming thing
For so many falls into its path
And can't break free

Prey

It was the dawn of day
I'd worked so hard the day before
This day I longed to enjoy
To the mall I rushed eager to be
Until confronted by an unfriendly three
I walked with eloquence proud to be
While being watched like prey from a tree
Swooping down to end my stay
Lord why does this happen so often today
I feel like a bird being chased by its prey.

Angry Feelings

Anger brings out the worst in us
It drains our strength
It steals happiness
It dims the light in our hearts
It blocks the precious gifts of God

Friendship

A Special Friendship

Though you're gone
Your memories live on
Memories of you
And the things we used to do
Times when we sat in the summer shade
Grooving to the music
Those from the olden days
Memories of us sharing
The many difficulties in life
You'd say don't worry
Everything will be all right
Tomorrow will be a brighter day
Hang high and pray.
Though you're gone
Those memories will live on
That friendship we knew
Lived between us two
So, when you cross that threshold
Into that brand-new life
Just remember that old saying
Everything will be alright

A Son's Love

Dad you are
A man of essence and equality
The kind of man
You taught me to be
at times when faced with adversities
You showed strength
That encouraged me
You taught me so much in life
Rules to follow
To do what is right
I am so proud to be
A man of equality
Such love will always be
For because of you
Is because of me

A Special Grandson

God knew this day would be
and so, he blessed the coming of a special grandson
one who would glorify his holy name
one who would do for other's
and expect them to do the same.
one who would speak words of righteousness
one chosen and loved by thee
Thank you, Lord,
For the gift to lead
A call to righteousness
when our directions become hazed
so far from God's saving grace
My God what a blessing
A special grandson
whose life I will share
one who warms the heart
and walks the narrow path.

A Life Time

My life changed
with the echoing of your cry
That special day
as I waited with hours passing by
You came
and I knew
it would never be the same because of you God gave
and we adored
a grandson
soon to be a man
yes, I see
I am proud
of this person a man to be
and with the happiness that you bring
an echoing cry, long since the day gone by
blessed
by God
who knows you so well
my grandson
now 16
I see the love of God through you

Happy Birthday   Alvin 2

A Friend Forever

On a warm summer day
not many years ago
a friend came to visit
this friend I did not know
He came and stood beside me
as my eyes filled with tears
He said not to worry
he said not to fear
I wondered how he knew
the sadness I encountered
His presences I felt
seemed stronger than a mountain
And though I never saw his face
happiness filled my heart
replaced by sadness
A gift He left to pass along
I'm with you every day
even until the end of time
my love for you will stay.
Then he turned and walked away
this friend I never knew
now lives inside my heart
and I see life
with a different view.

Nature

Purple Petals

Looking out my window
drawn to my view
a patch of purple petals
as if they had a clue
Its petals were so small
with stems about to fall
they seemed just to say
I'm glad I came your way.
We rise to the morning sun
and return when noon has come
We live until life is done
we love because your heart we've won.

Beautiful Rose

From the dew on the freshest rose
so beautiful to see
its fragrance so lovely
its existence called by thee
To warm the hearts of many
whose love is
Felt within
And those who gives such a gift
to a special friend

Little Red Bird

Little red bird
High up on a limb
What is it that you sing
What joyful sound you bring
Such happiness I feel
Early in the morning.

An Old Tree

An Old tree
Lost in time
Carried a secret
Of a life
Left behind
No one knows
How it came to be
Just a beautiful lady
Carved in the tree
waiting and longing
Wanting to be free

The Rarest Rose

It comes with the burst of the morning sun
It's petals so beautifully designed
It's fragrance so wonderful
The rarest rose, so divine
And as I lift it from its stem
A vision came to mind
The times you gave words of wisdom
O what a golden time.
Your words meant so very much to me
They helped me along the way
In times of uncertainty
Your words drove fear away
You were there to listen
From a heavy heart I was set free
Like the rose
Such beauty in all I see
Such joy in your presence
O loving
Mother
How special you are to me.

Holidays

A Savior Is Born

May The trueness of Christmas
fill every heart and every home
May we praise the very reason
this day a Savior born
May we ring in the season
with joyful songs
May God bless us with peace and propriety
each day the whole year long

A Mother's Love

Full of joy and peace
whose love is unconditional
with patience
you taught me to be
a mother and friend
how proud to have
the greatest mother of all

HAPPY MOTHER'S DAY!

Happy Father's Day

No card written could ever describe
Or express the man that God sees.
No one could ever know the joy
This great man brings.
When faced with tests he stood them all
His hands so busy he did not fall
He kept the faith with steady pace
His heart he gave to the gift of grace.
He stood the test he did not fall
God's hands blessed him, sustained him
Made him the best father of all.

A Thanksgiving Blessing

Our father
We give thanks in your holy name
For your countless blessings
You give to us each day
Giving hope to the hopeless
to families when times
Are gray
You give strength in times of weakness
And provide our daily bread
O the grace you give to thee
Your countless blessings you give so free
Especially this day
When families gather
to pray
Giving thanks
Giving praise
Giving hope
How we worship you O Lord

For all that you have done
as families gather together
with thanks, to the faithful chosen One

An Easter Blessing

Oh! what a blessing
And the joy that it brings
Singing songs of praise
He is risen from the grave.
Oh! what a blessing
No greater love than thee
His holy life he gave
To set the captive free
Oh! what a blessing
To sing and praises his name
His mercy is forever
Our failures he holds no blame
We celebrate this day
For all that he has done
Let the whole world know
Of the holy risen One.

Christmas Rap

Old St. Nicholas is coming to town
Not a single eye open can be found
Leaving joy under the Christmas tree
Lots of presents for you and me.
Rocking around the Christmas tree
Lots of fun for you and me
From early morning
till late at night,
fun more fun no end in sight.
Rocking around the Christmas tree
Here comes Santa one two three
can you hear it?
can you hear it?
Santa Claus is coming to town.

What A Savior

Oh, what a savior
Whose blessings never end
In times of weakness
He is our greatest friend
He calls us to himself
At times so unaware
And tells us how he loves us
And shows how much he cares
When we are lonely
Just listen and hear his voice
He gives us words of wisdom
And guides us from the fall
Oh, what a savior
His blessings never end
Great in all his mercy
Our God who calls us friend

The Cross

When we look to the cross
His face we cannot see
he is not there
He died for you and for me
When we look to the cross
The pain he must have known
His great scarred hands
Nailed to the tree
On his head a crown of thorns
So very hard to bear
his mother looking on
His pain she could not share
Though she knew in her heart
One day he would surely be
Sitting at the right hand of the Father
To become the King of Kings
When we look to the cross
How blessed we all must be
Our Lord our Savior
By the shedding of his blood
He has set the captives free

The Joys Of Christmas

May the joys of Christmas
fill every heart in every home
May we praise the very reason
this day a Savior born
May we ring in the season
with joyous heart felt songs
May God bless you with peace and propriety
each day the whole year long

Merry Christmas and a Happy New Year

Rejoice

Lift every voice
Higher than the mountain tops
Over oceans
Over seas
To the heavens above
O magnify the king
He has risen from the grave
Rejoice
Rejoice
Bless his holy name
From sin we've been set free
It was promised
on Calvary
When they nailed him to the tree
The blood he shed for you and me
Rejoice
Celebrate the holy king
O the price he surely paid
He is worthy of all praise.

Children

Memories In The Sand

Today I watched the children play
In sand they built memories to stay
A castle for two
An ocean so blue
How happy they seemed
As their little eyes gleamed
With sand they built a little boat
A pirate in a red and white coat
Who helped them cross the deep blue sea
Where little ones play
On the shore so free

A Little Boy's Wonder

One hot summer day
With a clear blue sky
A little boy points to the birds up high
Their wings stretched out so very wide
clouds that formed mountains with shoes
Flowers wake to the morning sun
Ants whose work is never done
On a hot summer day with a clear blue sky
A little boy wonders and seeks reasons why

Seasons

Summer Time

Summer time
Under a weeping willow tree
We sat feeling the breeze
Across our face
Sweet kisses
A warm embrace
Our hearts racing like never before
We became lovers
Forever more

Winter

Its days are cold and dreary
So few flowers bloom
The birds find a hiding place
the trees hang their branches in gloom
The snow comes
What a show, falling around
as children rush to play
Making angels on the ground
Winter
blankets gloves and hats
Coats on people,
even on dogs and cats
For a season
Then it is through
I see the first sign of spring
A bud peeking through

April Fool _____

If you look under the sofa
crawling up the living room wall
You'll see a big black _____
and hear it's long black _____
If you try to catch it
don't let him hear your feet
he's just my friendly _____
who knows it's time to eat.

Beauty Everywhere

When I was a little girl
I found beauty everywhere
To sit in grandma's old brown chair
so very big and soft,
the happiness I felt when I heard her gentle voice.
I found beauty in an old dark room
with the light from grandma's lantern
there I could pretend
no consequence there after
dressed in an old gray dress
and shoes that stood so high.
How great this made me feel
with grandma standing close by
When I was just a little girl
I found beauty everywhere
in grandma's house
an old dark room
and grandma sitting near.

Meet the Author

Dorothy A. Simms

Dorothy Simms was born in the month of August 71 years ago in La Plata, Maryland. Her parents, both now deceased, were very stern while raising them; with eleven children they had to be. Her home was always filled with laughter and though they may not have been rich Dorothy never felt poor because they made do with what they had. When asked what she wanted to be when she grew up Dorothy remembers only wanting to be a teacher. She remembers lining up the few dolls she had and reading to them.

In August of 1966, Dorothy married and then had two wonderful children. They are now and will always be the joys of her life. In 1967, she was hired as a Teacher's Assistant. It helped tremendously in raising her children to work and have a second income. It also helped her gain the experience needed to become a teacher and then Director. When Dorothy attended college to earn her degree and pursue a career in education, she did not realize she had been blessed with the gift of writing.

In 1989, that changed. That year her writing gift, which had been there all the time, was sparked by a news report that upset her to the depths of her soul. People with gold on their minds had killed others who wore gold around their necks and that gold became the beginning of her writing journey. Her first poem, *Stolen Hearts and Minds*, has multiplied into over 300, with many in this volume.